SAVAGE NATURE

Extreme Adaptations

Louise Spilsbury

FRANKLIN WATTS
LONDON·SYDNEY

Franklin Watts
First published in Great Britain in 2016 by The Watts Publishing Group

Credits
Produced by Calcium
Series Editors: Sarah Eason and John Andrews
Series Designer: Paul Myerscough
Picture researcher: Rachel Blount

Photo credits: Cover: Shutterstock: J Reineke; Inside: Dreamstime: Allocricetulus 30, Daniel Bellhouse 19, Christian C. Berclaz 18, Bevanward 32, Dennis Donohue 27, Bonnie Fink 42, Jnjhuz 3, 40, Chris Kruger 11, Chris Moncrieff 23, Orchidart 20, Pamela Peters 4, Stephan Pietzko 41, Schnappschusshelge 15, Mogens Trolle 10, Twildlife 36, Nick Vermeulen 22; Shutterstock: Henk Bentlage 14, Mircea Bezergheanu 43, Nick Biemans 44, Ryan M. Bolton 5, Chantelle Bosch 33, Tony Brindley 25, Critterbiz 9, Curioso 17, Agustin Esmoris 29, Sergey Krasnoshchokov 24, D. Kucharski K. Kucharska 34, Petr Malyshev 38, Petrova Maria 39, Silviu Matei 37, Matteo Photos 21, MattiaATH 1, 16, Dave Montreuil 6, 7, Sari ONeal 13, Oksana2010 12, Pablo Mendez Rodriguez 35, Becky Sheridan 45, B G Smith 28, Gleb Tarro 26, John Tunney 8, Feng Yu 31.

Dewey number: 578.4
ISBN: 978 1 4451 4568 6

Printed in China

Franklin Watts
An imprint of
Hachette Children's Group
Part of The Watts Publishing Group
Carmelite House
50 Victoria Embankment
London EC4Y 0DZ

An Hachette UK Company
www.hachette.co.uk

www.franklinwatts.co.uk

Contents

Chapter 1

Hunting tactics

A lioness crouches behind the tall grass, her eyes fixed on the gazelle. Her powerful muscles are tensed, and her sharp teeth and claws are at the ready. If the attack fails, the lioness and her cubs will go hungry. If the gazelle fails to escape, by running fast and leaping high, it will die. They, like all animals, have special adaptations to help them to succeed and survive.

Ways to adapt

A lioness's fur is coloured to camouflage her against the dry grasses where she lives. This is a physical adaptation. She often crouches low and sneaks up on prey before chasing it. This is a behavioural adaptation. Most animals use both types of adaptation to get shelter, escape danger, find mates or locate food. In this book, we explore behavioural adaptations, and in this first chapter we look at the hunting tactics animals use to catch food.

Lions are heavy and cannot run fast for long. So they stalk their prey before pouncing.

Alligator snapping turtle

The alligator snapping turtle is the largest freshwater turtle in North America. With its heavy, armoured body, it weighs about 77 kg. This brute of a turtle is big and powerful but not fast enough to chase its fish prey. Instead, it lies patiently in wait in the murky waters where it lives with its jaws wide open, striking only when its prey comes close.

Extra extreme

The alligator snapping turtle has a smart way to attract fish – a built-in lure. A pink piece of flesh sticks out from its tongue, looking a bit like a worm. When a fish swims in to investigate, the turtle snaps and grabs it.

Alligator snapping turtles have powerful jaws that can crunch through bone.

Black heron

The black heron is sometimes called the umbrella bird because it stands in shallow water with its wings spread above its head like an umbrella. Why does it behave like this?

Stealthy stabber

The black heron uses this umbrella as a stealth tactic so it can stab fish and then eat them. The umbrella shades the water, which reduces glare from sunlight overhead so the heron can see what is moving under the surface. The shade also attracts fish and amphibians hoping to hide in the darker waters. A black heron walks slowly around the marshy place where it lives and forms the umbrella for just a few seconds before moving on and repeating the behaviour.

Without its umbrella, a black heron would find fewer prey.

Standing tall

Some fish-eating birds catch their prey by diving under the water. The black heron, however, lives on lakes where the water is too shallow to do this. It instead walks through the water on long legs that also allow it to stand high enough above the surface to get a good view of any movement from likely prey. The heron usually hunts on its own during the day, particularly around sunset, when there is less reflection on the water. It then gathers with hundreds, sometimes thousands, of other herons at night to rest.

Herons have a sharp, dagger-shaped beak to pierce or grab prey, which they then usually swallow whole.

Extreme!

Tempting toes

The black heron has some physical adaptations that help the umbrella stealth tactic. Its especially broad wing feathers are shaped to link together and stop any sunlight from passing through them. The bird also has yellow feet that it shakes underwater, which attracts the attention of passing fish.

Humpback whale

The 36-tonne humpback whale has a problem. This giant of the ocean needs to eat around 1,360 kg of food a day. However, by working in groups and using clever catching skills, the whales have found methods of filling up fast.

Food filters

Humpbacks are baleen whales. Instead of teeth they have long curtains of bristles, called baleen, in their jaws. They take a mouthful of water and use their giant tongues to push it back out through the baleen to trap any fish or krill, a kind of small shrimp, that the water contained. They then swallow the trapped food.

A humpback takes in huge mouthfuls of water and uses its huge tongue and bristly baleen to filter out the tiny fish it feeds on.

Humpbacks use 'bubble nets' to drive fish up to the surface. The fish are trapped by the bubbles and cannot escape.

Amazing air net

When there is little prey in each mouthful of water, humpbacks need to spend far more time and energy feeding than when the water is more bountiful. To get bigger mouthfuls of food, groups – known as pods – of humpbacks use 'bubble nets'. Whales find a school of fish and take turns diving up to 180 m to get underneath the school. They form a circle and blow air from the blowholes on their heads. The bubbles rise, forming a net of bubbles that traps the prey. Each whale then takes its turn swimming up inside the net to feast on the fish.

Extreme!

Mealtime methods

Humpbacks are not the only whales that hunt in pods. Sometimes killer whales make waves with their tails to wash resting seals off floating ice into the teeth of a waiting killer whale. Pods of their close relatives, dolphins, chase fish schools onto mud banks and lie in wait with mouths open as the panicking fish try to leap to safety.

Wild dog

African wild dogs live in sociable packs of between 6 and 20 family members. When they hunt together they can use their combined power to savage and kill animals much larger than themselves. They favour antelopes but sometimes hunt zebras 10 times the weight of one dog.

Meat-eating marathon

At the start of a hunt, the wild dogs in a pack circulate and howl. The adult dogs walk and then run towards a herd of potential prey. One animal, identified as weaker than the others, is targeted and the pack may chase it for up to 6 km. Some dogs run near the prey and others lag behind, saving energy to take over once the leaders tire. At the end of this marathon, the pack sink their teeth into the exhausted prey.

By working as a team, wild dogs can chase off scavengers such as hyenas (centre) that may injure them while trying to steal their prey.

The African wild dog has excellent eyesight, and big ears to listen to pack calls.

Dinnertime for dogs

Pack leaders usually let weaker adults eat first while keeping watch for hyenas. The dogs eat what they can and then return to the rest of the pack, including females with very young pups and other adults that babysit older youngsters. These pack members whine and beg for food and the hunters regurgitate meat from their stomachs for them to eat.

Extra extreme

African wild dogs can run at speeds of up to 56 kph – faster than Olympic sprinter Usain Bolt. The dogs can also maintain the speed for several kilometres. A wild dog pack searches for food over a wide area, which can measure as much as 2,300 km². That is bigger than the whole of London.

Chapter 2
Keeping safe

Animals that are hunted by other animals need ways to keep safe. Many animals have physical adaptations to protect them, like body colours or markings, called camouflage, that make them blend into the background of the habitat where they live. Animals have ways of behaving to protect themselves, too.

Take cover!

Different species of animal have different behavioural adaptations that keep them safe. When a hedgehog is threatened, it rolls itself into a tight ball. The spikes over its back then protect its soft stomach and nose. Rabbits run into underground dens when they hear predators, and cats climb trees to escape when they are chased. Living in groups, or herds, also protects animals. Rainforest chimpanzees, for example, live together so they can warn each other if they spot danger.

Hedgehogs roll into a ball to deter predators with their sharp spikes.

Playing dead

When an opossum is frightened, it freezes with terror. It falls to the ground on its side, with its legs stretched out, goes totally limp and stays still. When an animal runs, some predators get excited and want to attack. A motionless opossum does not excite their appetite, so they leave it in peace. Gradually the opossum comes round again and wanders off safely.

Extra extreme

Opossums can even fake illness to escape from predators. They build up a lot of spit, or saliva, that they drool from their mouth and even blow bubbles out of their nose. This makes it look as if they could be carrying a disease, so predators leave them alone.

Opossums may play dead for up to four hours!

Meerkat

Meerkats are small, furry animals that face constant danger because they have many predators. Birds of prey, such as eagles and hawks, hunt them from the air. Jackals, wild cats and big snakes hunt them on the ground. To keep safe, meerkats have developed clever ways of behaving.

Guard duty

Meerkats eat mostly insects, spiders and scorpions that they dig from under the ground. So, when they feed, meerkats cannot watch for predators. That is why they live in groups of up to 30 animals, called mobs. While most meerkats are feeding, one or two others act as lookouts. They climb trees or mounds of earth and stand tall, propped up on their stiff tails, watching out for danger from the air and on the ground.

Guard duty lasts about an hour before another meerkat takes its turn watching for predators.

Warning calls

If a guard spots a predator, it lets out a distinctive warning call. Instantly, all the meerkats race to the nearest entrance of their extensive underground tunnel network. If a predator is too close, meerkats dig quickly to create a cloud of dust in the hope that this will confuse the predator long enough to give them time to escape.

A meerkat has a keen sense of smell and sharp teeth to find and capture prey.

Extreme!

Sounds for safety

Meerkats make different sounds to mean different things. A meerkat's warning call sounds like a shrill bark. Meerkat guards make a different sound to tell the mob when the coast is clear, and their calls get louder and faster as a predator gets closer and closer.

Zebra

Zebras live on open grasslands in Africa, where lions, hyenas and other predators sneak up on these distinctively striped animals from behind the tall, dry grasses. To keep safe, zebras gather together in huge herds of hundreds or even thousands of animals.

Awake to dangers

Zebras are grazing animals, so they feed with their heads down. They raise their heads often to look and sniff for danger. In a large herd, that means there are many animals on the lookout, making it less likely a predator will be able to take the herd by surprise. At night, a zebra sleeps standing up only for an hour or so at a time, and only when a few other grazing zebras are awake, so there is always someone keeping guard.

Each zebra's stripe pattern is unique, like a human's fingerprints.

Extreme!

Confuse the captor

A zebra's stripes help to keep it safe, too. When zebras in a herd run away, the stripes make it hard for a lion to tell where one zebra ends and another begins. The lion gets confused and cannot work out which way each zebra is moving. This makes it hard for the predator to target a single zebra.

On the run

If a predator attacks, zebras run away fast in all directions. Some run in zigzag patterns to make it harder for attackers to catch them. Zebras will gather around a mother and baby from their herd to protect them from a pack of hyenas. They then kick out with powerful back legs to get rid of the snarling predators.

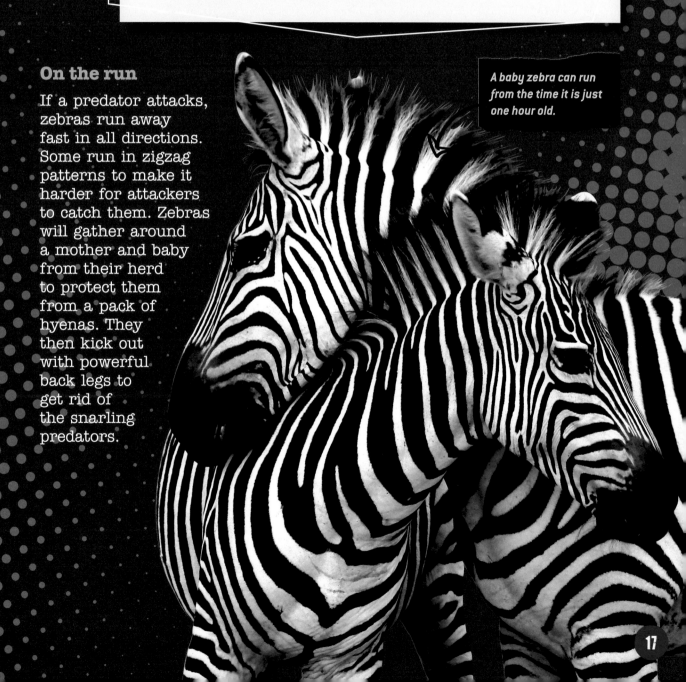

A baby zebra can run from the time it is just one hour old.

Chapter 3

Smart tricks

All animals need food to survive, and some have very clever ways of getting the food they need. Sea otters, for example, use stones as hammers to knock abalone shells off rocks and to crack the hard shells open so they can eat the animals inside. Chimpanzees are even more clever. They have developed a number of ingenious tools to help them to get their food and drink.

Super sponges and sticks

Thirsty chimps make sponges by chewing leaves into mush, and then dipping them into puddles of water. The sponges soak up the liquid, which the chimps then drink. Chimpanzees also use sticks and rocks to smash open tough fruits or hard nutshells. They then use smaller sticks to pick out the bits of nut left in the shell that they cannot reach easily with their teeth or fingers.

Chimpanzees are extremely clever and can come up with ways of behaving to get what they need.

Snacks on sticks

Chimpanzees also turn sticks into food-finding devices. They pick up a twig, rip off its leaves, break it to the right length and bite it into the best shape. Then they dip the stick into a termite nest or ant nest to fish for food, wiping the insects into their mouth. Chimps use stick tools as well to scoop honey from bees' nests to avoid getting stung.

Chimpanzees shape and break sticks to make tools for finding food.

Extra extreme

Crows know some smart tricks, too. They drop stones into water containers to raise the level of the liquid inside so they can reach and drink it. Carrion crows drop walnuts onto pedestrian crossings so cars drive over the shells and break open the nuts. The birds wait till the lights change colour and it is safe to cross before collecting their dinner.

Trap-door spider

Ambush attacks are the specialty of the trap-door spider. Rather than hunting down prey, this cunning creature makes a trap and lies in wait for its dinner to be delivered.

Setting the trap

To make its trap, the trap-door spider digs out an underground tunnel or burrow using fang-like mouthparts. Its jaws move up and down and are full of tiny spikes that help the spider to dig. Once the spider has dug a tunnel, it builds a door for the top from silk and earth. The trap-door is hinged on one side with silk so it opens and closes easily. The spider covers the door with bits of leaf, twig and rock to camouflage it.

The entrance to a spider's trap is almost impossible to spot unless the door is open.

Trap-door spiders use their burrows to ambush prey, hide from predators and raise young.

Ambush!

When an unsuspecting insect – or even a frog, mouse, baby bird or small snake – passes by, the spider feels the vibrations its movements make on the ground above. Then, as quick as a flash, the spider throws open the trap-door and grabs the prey in its powerful jaws. It pulls its victim back down into the burrow and stabs downwards with its sharp fangs to kill the prey.

Extreme!

Spider nursery

Trap-door spiders have their young in burrows. A female lays her eggs there and covers them with silk to attach them to the burrow wall. She stays with the eggs until they hatch and then protects and feeds the young spiders. When they are about eight months old, the youngsters are ready to dig their own burrows and make their own traps.

Leafcutter ant

Leafcutter ants are simply amazing. They are the farmers of the insect world, creating fertile underground gardens that supply their huge colonies with food.

Foliage farming

Colonies of leafcutter ants in Central and South America may contain millions of individuals. To provide food for this huge number of hungry mouths, thousands of ants march out from their nest to collect leaves. They use their jaws to cut off pieces of leaf and carry these back. Deep inside the nest, ants chew the leaves into a pulp and release substances that encourage fungi to grow on it. Other ants tend the fungi garden, making sure it stays clean and grows well. Then the ants eat the fungi and feed it to the young larvae in the nest.

Leafcutter ants have powerful jaws that vibrate 1,000 times per second to clip off pieces of leaf.

Each tiny leafcutter ant can carry a load more than 50 times its own body weight. The amount of leaves cut from rainforests by these tough insect weightlifters adds up to about 15 per cent of all the leaves that rainforests produce.

Jobs for all

The secret of the leafcutter ant colony's farming success is teamwork. Different ants in the colony do different jobs. Soldier ants defend the colony with their huge jaws. Worker ants collect the leaves, tend the gardens, and feed and care for the larvae. There are also some ants that release a substance that acts as a pesticide to kill off a particular mould that can damage the fungus gardens. And there is even a group of tiny worker ants that ride on the backs of the leaf collectors to defend them from attack by predator flies.

To find the right kind of leaf, a leafcutter ant may travel hundreds of metres – a long way for an ant.

Chapter 4
Surviving winter

When the weather gets cold, we put on jumpers and coats and turn up the heat to keep warm. Animals behave in a number of different ways to stay warm and survive the challenges of the extreme cold and lack of food they face in winter.

Caribou migration

When winter comes, some animals move to warmer places to avoid the cold and to find food. This behavioural adaptation is called migration. Caribou are large deer that migrate every year between forests and the tundra, in huge herds of up to half a million animals. The round trip can be as long as 4,800 km. The tundra is very cold, harsh and windy during the winter, so caribou migrate to forests further south, where the weather is milder and there is more food.

Caribou have hooves that can spread out on snow or soft ground to stop them from sinking.

Seasonal foods

Caribou herds split up in winter, and the animals spend their time feeding in forests. During the winter, they eat mainly lichens called reindeer moss, which they reach by digging under the snow. In spring, the caribou gather together in enormous herds to migrate north to the tundra. Throughout the summer they eat grass, leaves and buds. In autumn, they gather together again to migrate back to the forests.

Extra extreme

The Arctic tern makes an incredible return trip of around 71,000 km between the North and South Poles each year. The seabird flies between breeding grounds in Greenland in the Arctic and the Weddell Sea on the shores of Antarctica. By the end of its lifetime, one of these far-flying birds can travel the equivalent of three round trips to the moon.

Arctic terns catch fish such as sand eels for themselves and for their chicks to eat, and to fuel a monumental migration.

Grizzly bear

Grizzly bears are huge animals anyway, but during the late summer and the autumn they gain even more weight. Grizzlies eat as much as they can and pile on the kilos because they need to build up large amounts of body fat. This allows them to survive in their dens during their winter sleep, called hibernation.

Digging a den

Grizzly bears live in the mountains of North America, where winters are cold and the berries, plant roots and small animals that these bears eat are scarce. So they find or make large, safe dens to rest in until spring when food is plentiful again. A den can be a rock cave, tree hollow or a hole in a hillside or under tree roots.

Grizzlies stand in rivers to catch salmon migrating inland from the sea. Eating oily salmon fattens up bears quickly.

Large adult grizzly bears can be about 2.5 m long and weigh around 400 kg.

Deep sleep

During its winter hibernation, a grizzly bear's heart rate slows down, its temperature drops and it goes to sleep. To stay alive, the bear's body breaks down the fat stored up in summer and autumn to use as food. By the time bears leave their dens in spring, they are very hungry and have usually lost up to one-third of their body weight. Mother bears are especially hungry and thin because they have been feeding babies in the den, too.

Extreme!

Clever cubs

Amazingly, grizzly bear cubs are born while their mothers are asleep in their winter dens. Females usually give birth to twins, and after birth the two cubs crawl to their mother's tummy to snuggle into her fur for warmth and feed on her milk – called suckling. The mother stays asleep while the cubs feed and grow, getting ready to follow their mother outside the den when spring comes.

Pika

Animals that live in places where summer growing seasons are short and winters are long often store food. They collect and store it somewhere safe to eat during the barren winter, when resources are low. The pikas of western North America are small, furry mammals that live in the mountains and spend a lot of their time foraging for food.

Building food supplies

Pikas scurry about rocky hillsides during the daytime gathering green plants like grasses, weeds and tall wildflowers that are plentiful in spring and summer. They eat some and make piles of extra food that they lay out in the sun. The sun's heat dries the plants, which stops them from going mouldy. Then the pikas carry the food into their dens in the rocks and store it until winter.

Pikas gather food in summer, when a lot of grasses and flowers grow in the mountains.

Winter wanderings

Pika fur gets thicker in winter to help keep in the warmth, but pikas still spend most of the winter inside their dens to avoid the freezing cold and the biting winds. They eat the dried grasses they have stored to survive and only venture out to forage when the weather is good or if their food supply runs low. Then the pikas gather foods such as lichen and cushion plants, which still grow in winter.

Nut knowledge

Squirrels sort the acorns that they collect for winter before hiding them in the ground or in the hollows of trees. In North America, squirrels eat the tastier nuts from white oak trees first and then store the acorns of red oak trees as they taste a little bitter but keep well.

Squirrels collect and hide hundreds of acorns in underground stores. They remember where the stores are and defend them from other squirrels.

Chapter 5

Escaping the heat

Animals can become weak and ill, and even die, if they get too hot and do not have enough water to drink. Some animals have to take drastic measures to stay cool and survive the extremes of very hot, dry climates.

Cool behaviour

Some animals use the heat to cool themselves. Kangaroos lick their forearms so hot air evaporates the spit and takes some heat from the blood under their skin. Other animals go to extreme lengths to conserve water. Kangaroo rats, for example, produce bone-dry faeces and only a tiny amount of highly concentrated urine. Many animals just get out of the way in the hottest times. Some, such as the little hopping jerboa that lives in deserts, are nocturnal, meaning they are active only at night, when temperatures are cooler.

The jerboa comes out at night to look for food, using its big eyes and ears and long whiskers to see, hear and feel in the dark. It gets water from the plants and insects it eats.

Burrowing owl

Unlike most owls, tiny burrowing owls live on the ground, some of the time in burrows. Staying underground in the hottest part of the day stops them from getting too hot and keeps them safe from predators such as hawks. Burrows are also safe places to rear young owls. Burrowing owls may dig their own nests, but quite often they save their energy by taking over a hole left by a prairie dog or armadillo.

A female burrowing owl has up to 12 young at a time that live in the safety of the burrow she digs.

Extra extreme

It might sound disgusting, but a burrowing owl collects and smears mammal poo around its burrow entrance. This attracts dung beetles, which are one of the owl's favourite snacks. There are also many other things on an owl's menu, from lizards and scorpions, to doves and mice.

Sidewinder snake

In the deserts of the United States and Africa, j-shaped marks left in the sand give a clue as to how sidewinder snakes deal with their extreme environment. It is all about keeping their body off the baking-hot sand.

Desert dances

Sidewinders live in deserts where daytime temperatures are usually above 40 °C. To avoid dragging the whole of their belly – which is up to 76 cm long – over the burning-hot sand, the snakes loop and raise their body into waves so that just two short sections of it touch the sand at any time. They then push against these points to move sideways. When not moving, the snakes quickly burrow down under the desert surface to cooler sand or dive into the nearest animal burrow for shade.

The sidewinder's special way of moving leaves curvy marks in the sand.

Heat seeker

At night, desert temperatures plummet and sidewinders go hunting on the cooling sand. They use special pits between their eyes and nostrils to sense heat given off by their favourite prey – rodents. Sidewinders approach silently in the dark and in the blink of an eye their large, curved fangs flick forwards and jab into their prey. The fangs inject venom, a kind of poison, from glands in the snakes' head. This stops prey from moving, so the snakes can stretch their jaws wide and swallow it whole.

Extreme!

Reptile rattle

A sidewinder has a built-in sound effect to scare off predators such as hawks and owls. The rattle at the end of its tail makes a hiss or buzz that tells predators it is a poisonous snake. The rattle is made from rings of keratin – the same material that our fingernails are made from – that scrape together when shaken.

Spadefoot toad

The spadefoot toad is a golf-ball-sized amphibian that remains buried under hot desert sand for months until the first signs of rain. Then it emerges, breeds, feeds and buries itself before the soil dries up again.

Rain alert

Spadefoot toads spend most of the year in a trance in underground burrows. This slow-motion existence, where the toads neither feed nor drink, is called estivation. Yet they still listen for the falling raindrops or vibrations of thunder that mark the start of the rainy season. Then the toads wake and burrow upwards. The males start to bleat to attract females to mate, and the females lay hundreds of eggs in temporary ponds formed when it rains.

Rain is heavy and infrequent where spadefoots live. So they have to dig to the surface fast while the ground is soft.

Extra extreme

Hurried meals

Once spadefoot tadpoles hatch after it rains, they need to get enough food to change into toadlets before the pools they live in dry up. The tadpoles graze on moss, water fleas and anything else they can find. Toadlets and adults hop around to also find food in a hurry. They flick out their tongue to catch termites, grasshoppers and spiders. Some eat all they need to survive estivation in just one sitting. The toads then take a big drink and burrow downwards once more.

When temperatures are very high and pools are drying up fast, some spadefoot tadpoles become cannibals. They develop an oversized head, strong jaw muscles and a beak-shaped mouth to eat smaller tadpoles. However, cannibal tadpoles do have some table manners – if other toad species are in their pool, they eat them first.

Spadefoot toads use their large front feet and sharp spade-like growths on their rear feet to dig tunnels into the ground.

Jackrabbit

Jackrabbits are large hares with enormous ears and hind feet. These features help them to cope with the heat of the day and listen for predators. However, their ability to survive relies on them being most active under the cover of darkness.

Night-time nibbler

Jackrabbits are active after dusk, when the temperature drops in the dry shrublands of North America they inhabit. They see well at night, and their giant ears hear even the quietest rustle that could signal danger. Jackrabbits use their heavy-duty front teeth to graze on anything from grasses to twigs. The plants are also their source of water. By day, jackrabbits snooze or lie still, crouched flat in shady hollows under bushes.

Having eyes on the sides of its head allows a jackrabbit to see all around and spot danger from every direction.

Jackrabbits hop along on their 30-cm long hind feet quicker than the fastest human sprinter can run.

Round-the-clock dangers

If a jackrabbit makes a wrong move during the day, a jackal, eagle or hawk could pounce. At night, owls are the main danger. To survive, jackrabbits flee fast, their hind legs pushing them along with powerful hops. They can leap more than 3 m high and cover the ground at up to 64 kph. However, it is not all about speed. Jackrabbits also run in zigzags and alternately put up one ear and then the other to flash a black-and-white pattern. These behaviours can confuse their pursuers.

Extreme!

Helpful heartbeat

When jackrabbits are hidden but know predators are close by, they can slow their heartbeat so their breathing cannot be heard. An instant before they start running for their life, their heart rate shoots up three times faster than normal and they are ready to take evasive action.

Chapter 6

Making shelters

Animals need shelters to keep them dry and warm in cold places, and cool and protected from sunlight in hot ones. An animal's shelter is also a place where it can hide from predators and have babies safely. Different animals have different ways of making their homes.

Do-it-yourself homes

Some animals have great building skills. Birds make nests from mud, feathers and plant materials to keep eggs and nestlings safe. Like birds, squirrels build large nests in trees out of leaves and twigs. Other animals simply make use of what is lying around them. The hermit crab is born without a shell, so it finds an empty shell to live in. When it grows too big for one shell, the crab moves to a bigger one.

Unless a hermit crab finds a shell that is the right size to live in, its soft body is open to attack by predators.

Animal weavers

Weaverbirds make the most extreme nests of all – beautiful and elaborate structures created by the careful looping and weaving of strands of grass or strips of leaves. A male weaverbird weaves the nest in the shape of an upside-down flask, with a narrow, downwards-facing entrance at the bottom so predators find it hard to get in. When a male is happy with his handiwork, he hangs upside down from it while calling out and gently flapping his wings to attract a female.

Sociable weaver nests are so well built that they can last for 100 years!

Extra extreme

Sociable weavers go a step further and weave one gigantic nest for all the birds in their colony. This is the bird equivalent of a high-rise block of flats. Groups of birds use twigs, grass and straw to make lots of rooms and many entrances inside the nest until it is so big that up to 100 families can live inside.

Beaver lodge

Beavers are the most famous builders of the animal world. These big rodents, each weighing around 27 kg, chop down trees and branches to construct giant homes, called lodges.

Chisel mouth

Beaver teeth are like two pairs of giant chisels. Beavers use them to strip bark and leaves from trees for food, and to cut down trees for lodge construction. Beavers drag some tree branches underwater and anchor them there. The branches serve as an emergency food supply in case the pond freezes over in the winter and the beavers cannot get to fresh trees.

A beaver can bite through a 13-cm thick aspen tree in 3 minutes!

Extreme!

Talented tail

Beavers have very wide tails. These are useful rudders when the rodents swim, and can be used to slap the water surface to warn others about approaching predators. On land, beavers use their tails to prop themselves up while they gnaw on trees. In the autumn, a beaver's tail fattens up and is a useful source of food energy over winter.

Beavers need good swimming skills to build lodges like these and to swim in and out of them.

Lodges and dams

Beavers build new lodges in the autumn. They gnaw on small trees to cut them down and use their mouth to drag the branches into messy cone shapes, lining the hollow centres with grass and mud. The lodges extend from lakes or pond banks into deeper waters, where the underwater entrances are located. The beavers go into these constructions to avoid predators such as wolves, to keep warm and to raise young. When beavers live by rivers, they may build branch-and-mud dams to block the flow of water and create lakes where they can more easily make lodges.

Prairie dog burrow

As their name suggests, prairie dogs live on prairies – in the United States, Canada and Mexico. Prairies are open areas of grassland with few trees or bushes for animals to shelter in, so prairie dogs work together to build incredible complexes of underground tunnels. These spread so far that they are known as 'towns'.

Building a community

Prairie dogs live together in groups, called colonies, which number hundreds or even several thousands of animals. A 'town' complex is made up of separate smaller areas in which different groups of prairie dogs live. Members of the colony all use their sharp, thick, black claws to help dig the burrows for their neighbourhood. Each burrow has at least two entrances or exits and consists of tunnels that lead to underground chambers or rooms.

Prairie dogs collect grass to line the nurseries and sleeping chambers inside their burrows.

Inside a burrow

Prairie dogs build the underground chambers for different purposes. They can rush into chambers near the surface to escape from predators. There are special toilet chambers where they deposit all their waste. Chambers deep below ground are for resting or sleeping, and some are lined with grass and used as nurseries, where baby prairie dogs are born and cared for.

Extreme!

Loud lookout

When prairie dogs leave their burrows to feed, one stays on top of the burrow mound to act as a lookout. If it spots a predator, it barks a warning to the others. The dogs have developed different sounds to mean different animals, such as 'hawk' and 'coyote'. When the warning is sounded, the dogs all run as fast as they can into the nearest burrow entrance hole.

Prairie dogs stand up on their back legs and open their mouth wide to warn other prairie dogs of any potential danger.

Chapter 7

Vital behaviours

We have seen how making complex burrows, playing dead, living in huge herds and many other extreme types of behaviour can help animals to survive. Such behavioural adaptations can be inherited or learnt from parents, who pass them on to offspring, generation after generation.

Time for school

Most young animals follow and watch their parents, and then through trial and error work out how to do things for themselves – and survive. This is how young chimps learn to fish for ants, and how young prairie dogs come to understand the warning signals that make their parents run for cover. Some animals, such as the raccoon, find new ways to adapt by themselves.

Many animals learn behaviours from their parents that help them to survive.

Extra extreme

Raccoon raiders

The raccoon is a great example of behavioural adaptation in action. As people have destroyed its habitat, this mammal has changed its diet and the places where it lives in order to survive. The natural habitat for raccoons is the forest, where they nest in trees and search for foods such as berries by day and fish at night. However, as people have cut down more and more forests, raccoons have adapted their behaviour. Today, many raccoons nest in attics, basements, garages and sheds, instead of trees. Rather than forest foods, they eat leftovers found in rubbish bins. Like all great survivors, they have adapted to changes in their environment to ensure their species continues to thrive.

Some animals, such as raccoons, rats and foxes, can adapt their behaviours quickly, which is why they are so successful. As people change the environment by cutting down trees or building on grasslands, animals that cannot adapt die out. Some scientists think that up to three of the planet's species die out every hour because of problems like habitat destruction and pollution.

Raccoons are very successful at adapting to a variety of places and challenges, even reaching and raiding bird feeders!

Glossary

adaptations physical or behavioural changes that help animals to stay alive in extreme conditions

amphibians animals that live on land and in water, such as frogs

behavioural adaptation a way of acting or behaving that helps a living thing survive

blowhole a breathing hole on the top of a marine animal's head

breed to reproduce or have young

camouflage colour or pattern that matches the surroundings and helps to hide something

colony a group of plants or animals growing or living in the same place

estivation to spend a hot, dry season in a sleep-like state

evaporate to change from a liquid into a gas

faeces the solid waste that leaves an animal's body

fungi (singular is fungus) a group of organisms that includes yeasts, mushrooms and moulds

herd a group of animals that live and move along together

hibernation the sleep-like state in which some animals spend winter

larvae (singular is larva) young animals, particularly insects, with different forms than adults

mammals warm-blooded animals that have hair or fur and feed milk to their young

migration the movement from one place to another to find food, breed or avoid extreme weather

nocturnal active at night

pesticide a substance that kills insects

physical adaptation a body part that helps an animal survive

pollution substances that poison or contaminate air, land or water

prairie an extensive, flat land that is covered mostly in grasses

predator an animal that kills other animals for food

prey an animal that is hunted by another animal for food

regurgitate to bring swallowed food up to the mouth again

rodents a group of small mammals, such as rats, that have strong gnawing teeth

scavengers animals that find and feed on dead animals or waste

school a large group of fish swimming together

species a type of living thing

suckling drinking milk from a female mammal's body

termite a small, pale, soft insect that lives in large colonies

tundra Arctic land where the ground is always frozen

venom poison produced by animals

For more information

Books

Amazing Animal Survivors (Read Me!: Animal Superpowers), Raintree

Evolution Revolution, Robert Winston, Dorling Kindersley

Super Survivors (Amazing Nature), Tim Knight, Heinemann

Survival: Animal Adaptations (Four Corners), Alice Cary, Longman

Websites

Read more about extreme animal survival and adaptation at:

www.bbc.co.uk/nature/adaptations

www.durrell.org/kids/fun-factsheets/adaptation-factsheet

http://education.nationalgeographic.co.uk/education/ encyclopedia/adaptation/?ar_a=1

http://mentalfloss.com/article/57204/20-amazing-animal- adaptations-living-desert

Note to parents and teachers
Every effort has been made by the Publisher to ensure that these websites contain no inappropriate or offensive material. However, because of the nature of the Internet, it is impossible to guarantee that the contents of these sites will not be altered. We strongly advise that Internet access is supervised by a responsible adult.

Index